King James Only Controversy

G. Michael Cocoris

Table Of Contents

Chapter 1

Introduction

In 1604, James I, the king of England, authorized a new English translation of the Bible. A group of fifty-four divines began work on the new Bible, which they completed in 1611. It is known as the Authorized or King James Version.

The King James Version of the Bible became the standard English translation until the discovery of two "earlier" Greek manuscripts motivated other English translations, beginning with the Revised Version (RV, 1881) and the American Standard Version (ASV, 1901). Throughout the 20th century, many other English translations followed, including the Revised Standard Version (RSV), The New American Standard Bible (NASB), The New International Version (NIV), the New King James Version (NKJV), and the English Standard Version (ESV). Some say there are now more than 200 English translations. With so many English translations available, the question is, "Which translation should I use?"

Some Bible-believing Christians say only the King James Version should be used. The King James Only movement is not monolithic; there are various versions of it. According to theologian James White, the King James Only movement is divided into five main groups (Wikipedia, "King James Only Movement").

1. "I Like the KJV Best."
2. "The Textual Argument." (The Hebrew and Greek textual base of the KJV is more accurate than the texts used by newer translations.)
3. "Received Text Only." (The Received Text a.k.a. "Textus Receptus," on which the KJV is based, has been providentially preserved.)
4. "The Inspired KJV Group." (The KJV itself was divinely inspired and, therefore, is as accurate as the original Greek and Hebrew manuscripts.)
5. "The KJV as New Revelation" a.k.a "Ruckmanism" after the late Florida pastor Peter Ruckman. (The KJV is an "advanced revelation," and when it differs from the original languages, it "corrects" them.)

Technically, the first three of these positions would allow an English translation other than the KJV. So, the KJV-Only question comes down to "Is the KJV inspired?" The "KJV is inspired" group (henceforth KJV-Only) insists that only the KJV is the *inspired* Word of God in English, that it is *without error*, and that *no other* English translation is to be used. Is the KJV inspired? Is it a perfect translation, meaning it is without error? Is it the final authority, that is, no other English translations should be used?

Summary: The KJV-Only position is that the KJV is the inspired, perfect, and the only authoritative English translation of the Bible.

Chapter 2

The Inspiration of The KJV

The first question concerning the King James only position is, "Is the King James version inspired?"

The Argument

The biblical argument for the inspiration of the King James Version is based on Psalm 12:6-7, which says, "The words of the LORD *are* pure words: *as* silver tried in a furnace of earth, purified seven times. Thou shalt keep them, O LORD, thou shalt preserve them from this generation forever." Those verses do not say anything about the King James Version, or, for that matter, any translation. So, how can the KJV-Only defenders use them to prove the inspiration of the KJV?

The proponents of the King James Version's inspiration claim that the expression "purified seven times" in Psalm 12:6 is a reference to the King James Version. Will Kinney argues that before the translation of the KJV began, 15 "rules" were established (see "A Brief History of the King James Bible" by Dr. Laurence M.

Vance, http://www.av1611.org/kjv/kjvhist.html). Rule 14 states: "These translations are to be used when they agree better with the Text than the Bishops' Bible: Tyndale's, Matthew's, Coverdale's, Whitchurch's [the Great Bible of 1540], Geneva." Kinney goes on to say, "That is a total of 6 specific previous English Bibles that (in the sovereignty of God) the 54 King James Bible translators were directed to use and compare for the 'purifying' and bringing forth the greatest Bible in history, and the only one still believed today by multiplied thousands of God's redeemed people to be the complete, inspired and inerrant words of the living God…. The King James Bible became the 7th purification of 'the words of the LORD."

Later, Kinney adds, "By the way, they started work on the King James Bible in 1604 and finished it in 1611. Seven years to bring it to its perfection." Moreover, he muses, "I think it is an interesting 'coincidence' to see that in creation events recorded in Genesis chapter One, six times God said 'it was good' – Genesis 1:4, 10, 12, 18, 21, and 25. But the seventh time He said 'it was very good' – Genesis 1:31 – 'And God saw everything that he had made, and, behold, it was very good.' We also see that God Himself did not bring forth the completed creation in a single day, but rather He took six days to progressively bring it to completion and then rested in His finished work on the seventh day. Just another 'coincidence', I suppose" (see Kinney's complete article at www.brandplucked. webs.com/7purificationsofwords.htm).

Advocates of the KJV's inspiration also point out that Psalm 12:7 says God *preserved* His words. Stewart says, "If God has kept His promise to PRESERVE His Word (and He has!), then those

Words must also maintain their inspiration" (David J. Stewart, http:// jesus-is-savior.com/Bible/inspired_or_preserved.htm; the word in all capitals is his). Simply put, the argument is that God promised to preserve His Word and *inspiration indicates preservation.*

To sum up, the biblical argument for the inspiration of the KJV says that since Psalm 12:6 is a reference to the King James Version ("purified seven times"), when verse 7 says God preserves His words, it is saying God preserved the King James Version, which means the King James Version is inspired.

The Answer

In the first place, the expression "purified seven times" in Psalm 12:6 does not refer to the KJV. "Purified seven times" means that the silver has been purified seven times; it is the purest silver. As MacDonald explains, "purified seven times—in other words, like the purest silver known. There is no deceit, no flattery, no double meaning, no error in God's words. They can be fully trusted." Ross puts it like this: "What God says is true (flawless; cf. Ps. 18:30) and reliable. His words are not tainted with deceit and false flattery (in contrast with the wicked's words, Ps. 12:2-3) but are fully dependable" (Ross).

In the second place, Psalm 12:7 says nothing about the preservation of God's words. Granted, the *English* translation of Psalm 12:6-7 appears to be saying that God preserves His *words* (verse 6 says the *words* of the Lord are pure and verse 7 says He preserves *them*), but the Hebrew text indicates that the term "them" in verse 7 is not referring to the *words* of the Lord in verse 6. The Hebrew word translated "them" in verse 7 is masculine and the Hebrew term translated "words" in verse 6 is feminine. Therefore, "them" (masculine) cannot refer to the words (feminine) of the Lord. In the context of Psalm 12, "them" in verse 7 refers to the poor and needy in verse 5.

Gill says, "Thou shall keep them, O Lord, [does not refer to] the words before mentioned [12:6] … for the affix is masculine and not feminine; not … God has wonderfully kept and preserved the sacred writings; and he keeps every word of promise which he has made, and the doctrines of the Gospel will always continue from one generation to another; but the sense is, that God will keep the poor and needy, and such as he sets in safety."

Calvin says, "Some give this exposition of the passage, *Thou wilt keep them,* namely, *thy words;* but this does not seem to me to be suitable. David, I have no doubt, returns to speak of the poor, of whom he had spoken in the preceding part of the psalm."

Barnes says, "Thou shalt keep them. That is, the persons referred to in Psa. 12:5—the poor and the needy who were suffering from the wrongs inflicted on them. The idea is that God would guard and defend them. They were safe in his hands. Compare Psa. 37:3-7."

This is not to say that God did not preserve His Word. He did. It is to say that this is not what Psalm 12:7 teaches. There is no support in Psalm 12, or anywhere else in the Scripture, for the inspiration of the King James Version of the Bible.

In the third place, the translators of the KJV did not claim that what they wrote was inspired; in fact, they *denied* it. After an examination of their preface, Bill Combs writes, "The KJV translators deny that their translation is perfect (no errors) since perfection is only possible when men are under the direct, supernatural inspiration of the Holy Spirit" (Combs, www.dbts.edu/2012/04/25/is-only-the-king-james-version-the-word-of-god/). In other words, they are saying their translation was not perfect because it was not inspired.

It is deeply significant that the translators of the King James Version did not claim inspiration, because the authors of Scripture did. As I have written elsewhere, "The words 'God said' occur ten times in the first chapter of Genesis. Moses, the author of the first five books of the Bible, claimed God spoke to him (Lev. 1:1; etc.) and that God told him to write down what He said (Ex. 17:14; 24:2-4). When Moses died, God told his successor, Joshua, to hear and heed what Moses wrote (Jos. 1:7-8). The prophets in the Old Testament made similar claims (Isa. 1:1; Jer. 1:1; Ezek. 1:1; Hosea 1:1; Joel 1:1; Amos 1:3; Obad. 1; Jonah 1:1; Micah 1:1; Nahum 1:1; Hab. 1:1; Zeph. 1:1; Haggai 1:1; Zach. 1:1; Mal. 1:1). The prophets claimed God spoke to them and they spoke for God. The Old Testament, then, clearly claims to be the Word of God. It is said that such expressions as 'the Lord said,' 'the Lord spoke,' and 'the Word of the Lord came' are found 3,808 times in the Old Testament. Furthermore, the New Testament claims the Old Testament is the Word of God (Heb. 1:1; 2 Pet. 1:20-21). The New Testament also claims that it is the Word of God. As Moses and the prophets claimed to speak for God, so did Paul (1 Cor. 14:37), John (Rev. 1:10, 11, 19), and Peter (2 Pet. 3:1-2). Moreover, Peter acknowledges that Paul's writings were Scripture (2 Pet. 3:15-16) and Paul quotes Luke, calling what Luke wrote Scripture (1 Tim. 5:18)" (from G. Michael Cocoris, *Relating Doctrine to Daily Life*, pp. 86-87). The point is that the authors of inspired Scripture *claimed* they were writing inspired Scripture, whereas the translators of the KJV specifically denied that their work was inspired. In other words, the biblical concept is that authors of inspired Scripture are aware of it and say so. Since the translators of the KJV denied that what they were doing was inspired, it was not inspired, and to say that it is violates a biblical concept.

Finally, the original 1611 KJV contained the Apocrypha, books written between the Old and New Testaments. The Apocrypha was a part of the KJV for 274 years until it was removed in 1885. The books in the Apocrypha were not inspired. None of them was quoted as Scripture by Jesus, the apostles, or early church authors. Later, some of them were accepted as deuterocanonical by the Roman Catholic Church. *If the original 1611 KJV is inspired, the Apocrypha is inspired!*

Summary: The correct interpretation of Psalm 12:7, the translators of the 1611 KJV, and the presence of the Apocrypha demonstrate that the KJV is not inspired.

Chapter 3

The Perfection of The KJV

The defenders of the KJV-Only position insist that the KJV is perfect, that is, that it is without error. Is that true?

The Argument

One defender of the King James only position says, "Notice that God said His Word is 'pure,' as pure as silver refined seven times. (The number seven in the Bible represents *God's perfection*.) We have God's perfect Word in the English language in the King James Bible" (Stewart, http://jesus-is-savior.com/Bible/inspired_or_preserved.htm, italics his). Combs says, "KJV-only proponents deny that there are any errors in the KJV and insist that it cannot be improved upon" (Combs, www. dbts.edu/2012/05/29/churches-should-adopt-a-modern-version-of-the-bible/).

The Answer

The translators of the King James Version did not claim perfection. Combs stated, "The KJV translators deny that their own translation is perfect (no errors)" (Combs, www.dbts.edu/2012/04/25/is-only-the-king-james-version-the-word-of-god/). Furthermore, Combs points out that "Prior to the KJV, there had been many English translations of Bible: Wycliffe (1382), Tyndale (NT, 1526), Coverdale (1535), Matthew's Bible (1537), the Great Bible (1539), the Geneva Bible (1560), the Bishops' Bible (1568), and the Douai-Rheims (1609–10)" (from the article by Combs, http://www.dbts.edu/2012/04/16/the-preface-and-opposition-to-new-translations/).

Then, Combs adds, "The translators recognize that previous English translations are 'sound' presentations of the Word of God, but only a fool would think that any human or group of human translators could produce perfection. They acknowledge 'nothing is begun and perfected at the same time,' and later scholarship can improve on the work of previous translators. It is obvious the KJV translators would be horrified at the thought their work was perfect and would be the first to commend later improvements and corrections of their work" (Combs, www.dbts.edu/2012/05/02/is-the-king-james-version-the-final-authority/).

Another indication that the translators of the 1611 KJV knew that their translation was not perfect is that they included margin notes. They felt these notes were necessary because often they were unsure how a word or phrase should be translated (Combs, http://www.dbts.edu/2012/04/09/the-embarrassing-preface-to-the-king-james-version/). They not only used margin notes, but also used many of them. "Scrivener counted 6,637 in the OT, 1, 018 in the Apocrypha, 767 in the NT, for a total of 8,422.... Of the 767 notes in the NT, 35 are explanatory notes or brief expositions, 582 give alternative translations, 112 give a more literal rendering of the Greek than the translators judged suitable for the text, and 37 give readings of different manuscripts" (Scrivener, cited by Combs, http://www.dbts.edu/2012/05/09/marginal-notes-in-the-king-james-version/).

For example, the 1611 KJV text of Romans 5:7 literally reads, "For when we were in the flesh, the motions of sinnes, which were by the law, did worke in our members to bring foorth fruit vnto death." The issue is not the antiquated spelling of words such as sins, work, fourth, and unto, but the expression "motions of sinnes. The translators of the 1611 KJV put "motions of sinnes" in the text, but in a margin note said, "Gr. passions." In other words, in a margin note, the translators said that the Greek word means "passions," but they put "motions" in the text!

Still, another indication that the translators knew that their translation was not perfect is that they cited Augustine, who said a "variety of translations is profitable for finding out the sense of the Scriptures" (see Combs, http://www.dbts.edu/2012/05/09/marginal-notes-in-the-king-james-version/). They recognized the value of a variety of translations!

In their preface to the 1611 KJV translation, the translators said that, as a virtuous man may have many slips in his life, warts on his hand, and freckles on his face, a translation should not be denied to be the Word of God because of some imperfections and blemishes. They would consider a translation with numerous defects to still be called the Word of God. They cite the Septuagint, the Greek translation of the Old Testament, which the New Testament writers quote (Combs, http://www.dbts.edu/2012/04/25/is-only-the-king-james-version-the-word-of-god/; the text of what the translators wrote is after the "summary" at the end of this paper).

Summary: The translators of the King James Version recognized that the 1611 KJV was not perfect.

Chapter 4

The Final Authority of The KJV

The KJV-Only advocates claim that the 1611 KJV is the final English authority, meaning that no other English translation is needed or should be used.

The Argument

Will Kinney says, "The English of the King James Bible is the final written authority from God and the standard by which all other translations should be measured" (Kinney, https://brandplucked. webs.com/elevateenglishinsults.htm). He also says, "I am convinced God's pure, perfect, and preserved words in English are found only in the Authorized King James Bible" (Kinney, https://brandplucked. webs.com/). Combs says, "Since the KJV-only proponents insist that only the KJV is the Word of God in English, they are radically opposed to any English translation produced in the last 400 years" (from the article by Combs, http://www.dbts.edu/2012/04/16/the-preface-and-opposition-to-new-translations/).

The Answer

The problem with the position that the original 1611 KJV is the final English authority and an inspired, perfect Bible is that there are so many versions and variations of the original 1611 KJV! There were two different versions of the *original* 1611 edition. One is called the "He Bible," and the other is called the "She Bible." In the "He" version, Ruth 3:15 reads "he went into the city," and in the "She" version, Ruth 3:15 reads "she went into the city." These two 1611 editions differ in about 450 places (David Norton, *Textual History of the King James Bible,* pp. 173–79). Which "authorized" version is the "final authority?"

Two versions of the 1611 King James Version each claim their version is the authoritative version. Speaking as a member of one group, Verschuur proclaims, "The Elders of Victory Faith Centre, in their providentially appointed role as the Guardians of the Pure Cambridge Edition, have identified the exactly correct text of the Pure Cambridge Edition. The revelation of this is accepted by various sincere Christians around the world. God has raised up one edition of the King James Bible, one exact representative, one last, refined, purified, and unchanging text. This particular text can be vindicated at every point and should be accepted as the Word of God in English. No other set of words can deserve such a place of esteem or exaltation as the Pure Cambridge Edition. It bears the marks of its divine providence throughout it" (Matthew Verschuur, www.bibleprotector.com/THERE_IS_ONLY_ONE_ PURE_KING_JAMES_BIBLE.pdf, bold print his).

On the other hand, Oxford Press claims, "Oxford is proud to announce a limited edition of the 1611 text of the King James Bible, with real leather binding, gilt edging, ribbon marker, gift presentation plate, and protective cloth slipcase. This is the most authoritative edition of the King James Bible available. The text of the 1611 edition differs from modern editions of the King James Version in thousands of details, and this edition is the most authentic version of the original text that has ever been published. It follows the 1611 text page-for-page and line-for-line, reproducing all misprints rather than correcting them. The volume also reprints the large body of preliminary matter, which includes genealogies, maps, and lists of readings, as well as the translator's preface to the reader. The text features an easy-to-read modern font instead of the black-letter type of the original, with the exception of the original decorative letters and early page ornaments, which have been reproduced. The volume concludes with an essay by Renaissance Studies expert, Gordon Campbell, on the first edition of the King James Bible" (https://www.thekjvstore.com/oxford-1611-king-james-bible-400th-anniversary-edition.html). Which "authorized" version is the "final authority?"

Actually, there are more than two versions of the 1611 KJV. "The KJV has been revised numerous times. Corrections were made in 1612, 1613, 1616, and 1617; more extensive revisions followed in 1629, 1638, 1762, and 1769. It is principally the 4th major revision by Benjamin Blayney in 1769 that is in use today.

Rick Beckman lists some of the significant changes the 1769 KJV made to the 1611 KJV. In the list, the 1611 reading precedes the 1769.

- 2 Kings 11:10 – "in the Temple" vs. "in the temple of the LORD."
- Isaiah 49:13 – "for God" vs. "for the LORD."
- Jeremiah 31:14 – "with goodnesse" vs. "with my goodness."
- Jeremiah 51:30 – "burnt their dwelling places" vs. "burned her dwellingplaces."
- Ezekiel 6:8 – "that he may" vs. "that ye may."
- Ezekiel 24:5 – "let him seethe" vs. "let them seethe."
- Ezekiel 24:7 – "powred it vpon the ground" vs. "poured it not upon the ground."
- Ezekiel 48:8 – "which they shall" vs. "which ye shall."
- Matthew 14:9 – "the othes sake" vs. "the oath's sake."
- 1 Corinthians 12:28 – "helpes in gouernmets" vs. "helps, governments."
- 1 Corinthians 15:6 – "And that" vs. "After that."

"There are two versions of the KJV in use: the Oxford and the Cambridge editions. Some of the differences between them affect the meaning of the text as well. For example, here are a couple of Cambridge passages vs. their Oxford counterparts."

- Jeremiah 34:16 – "whom ye had set" vs. "whom he had set."
- 2 Timothy 2:2 – "heard from me" vs. "heard of me."

"One cannot help to wonder about KJV-onlyism in light of the above. Was the King James Version of 1611 perfect? If yes, why were there such substantial changes made to the text between then and 1769? By using a modern edition of the KJV, are not the onlyists admitting that the 1611 translation was flawed? Which edition of the KJV is perfect? Between 1611 and 1769, was there a perfect English translation? Why is the 1769 edition perfect? What about the more recent Comfortable Edition? If you believe that translations can be inspired or that the KJV is an advanced revelation of some kind, as some KJV-onlyists do, why did God take over a hundred years to continue to revise his 1611 work? Does God work on a trial-and-error basis? I think these are all legitimate questions. From my experience of being a KJV-onlyist, I always heard that there were no substantial differences between the 1611 and the 1769. It is often claimed, as I noted above, that only spelling & printing errors were fixed. But clearly, there were changes to the content as well. KJV-onlyists should be aware of these claims, especially if they've bought into the idea that there were no substantial changes" (Rick Beckman, https://www.rickbeckman. org/log/kjv-1611-vs-1769/).

After comparing the translation of more than two dozen passages between the 1611 KJV and a modern KJV, Combs concludes, "For KJV-only advocates to argue that they hold the 1611 KJV as their final authority is at best silly and ill-informed, and at worst, extremely dishonest" (Combs, http://www.dbts.edu/2012/05/02/is-the-king-james-version-the-final-authority/). Which "authorized" version is the "final authority?"

Summary: The many versions and variations of the original 1611 KJV prove that the original 1611 KJV is not the final authority in English translations.

Chapter 5

The Current Translation of The KJV

The current translation of the King James Version is a major issue in this controversy.

The Argument

All KJV-Only backers argue that only the *1611* KJV must be used. In their literature and lectures, over and over, they insist that *only* the *1611* KJV is the Word of God and, therefore, *only* the *1611* KJV is to be used today.

The Answer

The first practical problem with that position is deciding which original 1611 KJV edition is the inspired, perfect, final authority Word of God in English. As noted earlier, there are two original 1611 KJVs, and they differ at about 450 points.

Even after deciding which edition is the original 1611 KJV, the practical problem is reading it! The "old English" makes it difficult to read. For example, the letter "s" sometimes appears as "f." Psalms is spelled *Pfalmes* and Isaiah is spelled *Ifaiah*. There are other obstacles to reading the original 1611 KJV in Old English. Proverbs is spelled *Prouerbes* and Jeremiah is spelled *Ieremiah*. I speak from experience; I own a copy of the original 1611 KJV. In all the reading I have done of KJV-Only material, I never seen even one author use the original 1611 KJV. In my experience, they all, *without exception*, use the more current 1769 edition.

Reading the 1769 edition of the KJV in the 21st century is not without its problems. For starters, it uses the old English "thee's" and "thou's. The current text of 1 Corinthians 13:4 says, "Charity suffereth long, *and* is kind; charity envieth not; charity vaunteth not itself, is not puffed up." When people today hear the word "charity," their first thought is of giving money to the poor, not love in general. That is only the beginning.

The current KJV text of Romans 10:21 says, "But to Israel he saith, All day long I have stretched forth my hands unto a disobedient and gainsaying people." What does the word "gainsaying" mean? Who uses that word today? The Greek word translated "gainsaying" means "to speak against, contradict." A more accurate translation is "a disobedient and contrary people."

The current KJV text of Romans 1:13 says, "Now I would not have you ignorant, brethren, that oftentimes I purposed to come unto you, (but was let hitherto,) that I might have some fruit among you also, even as among other Gentiles." What does "let hitherto" mean? The Greek word translated "let" means "to hinder, prevent, forbid." Paul says that, often, when he purposed to come to Rome, but he was hindered. In 1611, "let" meant to hinder, but when people hear that word today, they think "permit," not "prevent."

The current KJV text of 1 Thessalonians 4:15 says, "For this, we say unto you by the word of the Lord, that we which are alive *and* remain unto the coming of the Lord shall not prevent them which are asleep." How did those who are alive at the coming of the Lord "prevent" those who are asleep ("asleep" here means "dead")? The Greek word translated "prevent" means "to come before, precede." Paul is saying that those who are alive at the coming of the Lord will not go before those who are dead. As he explains in verse 17, "Then we who are alive *and* remain shall be caught up together with them in the clouds."

The current KJV text of 2 Corinthians 6:11-12 says, "O *ye* Corinthians, our mouth is open unto you, our heart is enlarged. Ye are not straitened in us, but ye are straitened in your own bowels." What in the world does "straitened in us, but ye are straitened in your own bowels" mean? We do not talk like that today. That is not translating the Bible into the common language of people, which is what the translators of the KJV purposed to do. Their translation of that verse might have communicated in 1611, but it does not communicate to common people today. A modern translation reads, "You are not restricted by us, but you are restricted by your *own* affections."

There are many, many more such examples.

In their eleven-page preface to the 1611 KJV, the translators noted that the Roman Catholic Church had generally not allowed the Scriptures to be rendered into the common language of the people, but that, in His providence, God raised up individuals to translate the Old Testament Hebrew Scriptures into Greek (the Septuagint). Since Scriptures cannot be understood until they are translated into the common tongue, translation is a good thing (Combs, http://www.dbts.edu/2012/04/09/the-embarrassing-preface-to-the-king-james-version). In other words, the translators of the 1611 KJV recognized the need for a translation into the common language of the people.

Unfortunately, KJV-Only believers want to follow the outdated 1611 KJV, but not the advice of its translators. As the KJV was repeatedly updated from 1611 to 1769, we also need to be able to read the Bible in today's English.

Summary: The translators of the 1611 KJV recognized that the English translation of the Bible needed to be updated.

Chapter 6
Conclusion

Contrary to the KJV-Only advocates, who believe the 1611 KJV is the inspired, perfect (without error), and final English authority of the Word of God (no other translation is to be used), the Bible does not support such a position. Moreover, the translators of the 1611 KJV denied that what they did was inspired, recognized that it was not perfect, and acknowledged the need for ongoing changes and for a translation in the common language of the people.

The King James Translators

If the King James translators were alive today, they would NOT be KJV-Only believers. They would INSIST their translation of 1611 be improved. They would say that an errorless translation is impossible because the Holy Spirit does not superintend translators as the apostles were. They would go so far as to say that even if a translation had imperfections in it, it is still the Word of God! Here is what they wrote.

"We do not deny, nay, we affirm and avow, that the very meanest [worst] translation of the Bible in English set forth by men of our profession...containeth the word of God, nay, is the word of God:

as the King's speech which he uttered in Parliament, being translated into French, Dutch, Italian, and Latin, is still the King's speech, though it be not interpreted by every translator with the like grace, nor peradventure so fitly for phrase, nor so expressly for sense, everywhere.... A man may be counted a virtuous man, though he has made many slips in his life, (else there were none virtuous, for in many things we offend all) also a comely man and lovely, though he has some warts upon his hand, yea, not only freckles upon his face, but also scars. No cause, therefore, why the word translated should be denied to be the word, or forbidden to be current, notwithstanding that some imperfections and blemishes may be noted in the setting forth of it. For whatever was perfect under the sun, where Apostles or apostolick men, that is, men endued with an extraordinary measure of God's Spirit, and privileged with the privilege of infallibility, had not their hand? The translation of the Seventy [Septuagint] dissenteth from the Original in many places, neither doth it come near it for perspicuity, gravity, majesty; yet which of the Apostles did condemn it? Condemn it? Nay, they used it (as it is apparent, and as Saint Hierome [Jerome] and most learned men do confess), which they would not have done, nor by their example of using it so grace and commend it to the Church, if it had been unworthy the appellation and name of the word of God."

Conclusion: **The Preface of the 1611 KJV proves the KJV-Only position is wrong.**

A Personal Word

May I close with a personal word? I believe the Scriptures, the 66 books of the Bible, are inspired, and infallible. As for the Greek text, although I was taught the critical theory of the Greek New Testament in seminary, after I graduated, further research convinced me there are major problems with the critical text theory.

For approximately the first 25 years of my Christian life, I used nothing but the King James Version of the Bible. I admire its accomplishment and recognize that God has used it for centuries. I agree with George L. Robinson, who called the original King James Version of 1611 "a monumental, literary masterpiece, which, for the rhythm and cadence, will ever hold a very high place in the category of Bible versions" (Robinson, *Where Did We Get Our Bible?* cited by me in the forward to *The New King James Version in Great Tradition* by Arthur Farstad, p. ix). For the last 35 years, I have used the New King James Version. My reasons for using it rather than another translation are given in the paper I wrote, "The Translation of the Bible" (on my website, www.insightsfromtheword.com).

Please note, the New King James is a King James Bible! The New Testament is based on the Textus Receptus and, in many places, even retains the King James tradition. Arthur Farstad, the Executive Editor of the New King James translation project, says the New King James translation is the fifth major revision of the original Authorized Version (Farstad, p. 1).

By the way, Farstad points out that, as with the 1611 translation, the New King James took seven years to produce. Farstad also notes that in the name "New King James Version," the *New* can be stressed or the *King James* can be stressed. Farstad observes, "Both are true. If the latter is stressed too much, people will get the impression that the NKJV is difficult for most modern readers (as are earlier editions of the KJV in many places). If we overstress the *New* aspect, people get the idea that we have an entirely new version. This is not true. A sufficiently large part of the King James tradition is retained to merit our name. Yet there are enough changes in the work to make it much more readable" (Farstad, p. 2).

May I recommend that you consider using the NKJV, especially the *NKJV Study Bible*? It is one of the most accurate and exhaustive Study Bibles on the market. In the name of full disclosure, I should tell you that I wrote some of the notes for the *NKJV Study Bible*, but that is not the reason I am recommending it. Nor do I receive royalties; I was paid a stipend for the work I did.

One other word. This book has dealt only with the King James-Only position. The deeper and more technical issue is the Greek text of the New Testament. The King James Version and the New King James Version are based on the Textus Receptus. In the 19th century, two "earlier" Greek manuscripts, Vaticanus and Sinaiticus, were discovered. Those two manuscripts do not contain such passages as the last 16 verses of Mark, the incident of the woman taken in adultery, the end of the Lord's prayer, etc. All modern translations are based on those two manuscripts.

The first Greek text issue is the Textus Receptus versus Vaticanus and Sinaiticus. The vast majority of Greek scholars and Greek professors side with Vaticanus and Sinaiticus.

The second Greek text issue is that there are 6000 Greek manuscripts of the New Testament. The vast, vast majority of them are in basic agreement. That group of manuscripts has been called the Textus Receptus, the Traditional Text, the Majority Text, the Byzantine Text, and the Family 35 Text, but there are differences among them.

In my book, *The Greek Text Issue*, I have explained this technical and complicated subject, including a chapter on the differences that make a difference. In it, I demonstrate that Vaticanus and Sinaiticus are not the best manuscripts. I also explained the differences between the Textus Receptus, the Traditional Text, the Majority Text, the Byzantine Text, and the Family 35 Text. It is available on my website, www.insightsfromtheword.com, and at Amazon, and Barnes & Noble.

Summary: What the translators of the original 1611 KJV said in their Preface proves that the KJV-Only position is wrong and that the updated version of the KJV, namely, the New King James Version, should be used, since it is the latest version of the KJV.

In all of this discussion, we should not lose sight of the fact that what we all need to do is let the Word of Christ dwell in us richly (Col. 3:16) so that we will trust and obey the Lord.

BIBLIOGRAPHY

Barnes, Albert. Albert *Barnes' Notes on the Bible.* e-sword.net.

Calvin, John. The Epistles of Paul the Apostle to the Romans and to the Thessalonians. Translated by Ross Mackenzie. Edited by David W. Torrance and Thomas F. Torrance. Grand Rapids: Wm. B. Eerdmans Publishing Co., 1961.

Cocoris, G. Michael. *Relating Doctrine to Daily Life: An Explanation and Application of The Basic Doctrines of The Bible.* Santa Monica, CA: J & M Brothers Publications, 2026.

Farstad, Arthur L. *The New King James Version: In the Great Tradition.* Nashville: Thomas Nelson Publishers, 1995.

Gill, John. *John Gill's Exposition of the Entire Bible.* e-sword.com.

MacDonald, William. *Believer's Bible Commentary.* Nashville: Thomas Nelson Publishers, 1990.

Norton, David, *Textual History of the King James Bible.* Cambridge: Cambridge University press, 2005.

Ross, Allen P. "Psalms." *The Bible Knowledge Commentary: Old Testament*, pp. 779-899. Edited by John F. Walvoord and Roy B. Zuck. Wheaton: Scripture Press Publications, Victor Books, 1985.

About The Author

G. Michael Cocoris is a gifted communicator. He can make even complicated subjects simple, clear, and practical. His breadth of experience has allowed him to relate to a wide range of audiences.

Michael received a Bachelor of Arts degree from Tennessee Temple University, a Master of Theology degree from Dallas Seminary, and a Doctorate of Divinity from Biola University. He traveled the United States for over a dozen years as a speaker. He has also been a seminary professor, visiting lecturer, and world traveler, including hosting tours to Israel and China.

Michael has pastored three churches, including a rural church when he was in seminary, an urban church, the historic Church of the Open Door, first in downtown Los Angeles and later in Glendora, California, and a suburban church, the Lindley Church in Tarzana California, a suburb of Los Angeles. While at the Church of Open Door, he had a daily radio broadcast.

Michael has written numerous magazine articles, mainly for *Biblical Research Monthly*. He has authored a number of books, including *Seventy Years on Hope Street, A History of the Church of the Open Door; How To Live A Biblical Spiritual Life, Clarifying the Confusion; Repentance, The Most Misunderstood Word in the Bible; Evangelism: A Biblical Approach; The Salvation Controversy; Lordship Salvation: Is It Biblical?; The Books of the Bible, the Subject, Structure, Situation, and Significant Verses of Each Book; Psalms, A Song for Every Situation, Each Summarized on One Page; and Counseling Theories, A Biblical Evaluation.* In addition, he was a contributor to The *NKJV Study Bible* and *Nelson's New Illustrated Bible Commentary*.

Michael is the pastor of the Lindley Church in Tarzana, California. He and his wife, Patricia, live in Santa Monica, California.